10/13

iMath
Readers

Finding the Treasure:
Coordinate Grids

by Renata Brunner-Jass

Content Consultant
David T. Hughes
Mathematics Curriculum Specialist

NORWOOD HOUSE PRESS
Chicago, IL

Norwood House Press
PO Box 316598
Chicago, IL 60631

For information regarding Norwood House Press, please visit our website at
www.norwoodhousepress.com or call 866-565-2900.

Special thanks to: Heidi Doyle
Production Management: Six Red Marbles
Editors: Linda Bullock and Kendra Muntz
Printed in Heshan City, Guangdong, China. 208N—012013

Library of Congress Control Number: 2012949928

ISBN: 978-1-59953-573-9

Summary: The mathematical concept of coordinate grids is introduced as
five friends embark on a high-tech geochaching adventure, using a handheld
GPS device. Readers learn how to plot data points from a table, label ordered
pairs, and name coordinate points on a grid. Applied key concepts include
the x-axis, y-axis, x-coordinate, and y-coordinate. This book also features a
discovery activity, a connection to geography, and a mathematical vocabulary
introduction.

CONTENTS

Note to Caregivers:

Throughout this book, many questions are posed to the reader. Some are open-ended and ask what the reader thinks. Discuss these questions with your child and guide him or her in thinking through the possible answers and outcomes. There are also questions posed which have a specific answer. Encourage your child to read through the text to determine the correct answer. Most importantly, encourage answers grounded in reality while also allowing imaginations to soar. Information to help support you as you share the book with your child is provided in the back in the **Additional Notes** section.

Bold words are defined in the glossary in the back of the book.

Getting Into Geocaching

Geocaching is high-tech, outdoor treasure hunting. Players use small, handheld devices to locate treasure. These devices are called **global positioning systems (GPS)**.

Treasure hunts begin with a trip to an online site, where treasure locations are stored. Geocaches are located on all seven continents. There's also one on the International Space Station!

Players plug their GPS devices into their computers. They click a *download* button on the site to store treasure locations into the GPS. Then, the hunt begins. The GPS directs players to locations where they can find a hidden waterproof container, or **cache**. This is the "treasure" in a high-tech game of treasure hunting.

Some treasures are inexpensive, such as toys. Players can take what they find. But they must leave something in place of anything they take. That's because the real treasure isn't what's in the container. It's in playing the game.

The following story is about a group of friends—Gita, Hayden, Cara, Marcus, and Tom—who invented their own high-tech treasure hunt one summer. They took turns making maps, writing clues, and hiding caches for the others to find.

What's on the Grid?

Grids are all around us. Cities and farms are often laid out in rectangular blocks. A solar array looks like a grid of solar panels. And maps! Whether we're looking online, at a GPS device, or at a printed map or globe, all maps are based on grids.

Gita, Hayden, Cara, Marcus, and Tom created a geocaching game. They put **coordinate grids** on their maps. They used these grids to create clues for their treasure hunts.

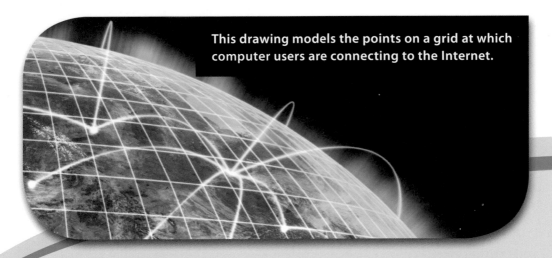

This drawing models the points on a grid at which computer users are connecting to the Internet.

A coordinate grid is drawn on a 2-dimensional, or flat, surface. It is made up of two number lines. One number line is horizontal, or going side to side. The other number line is vertical, or going up and down. The two number lines are **perpendicular**, meaning they form a right, or square, corner where they meet.

The horizontal number line on a coordinate grid is called the *x*-axis. The vertical number line is called the *y*-axis. The point where the two number lines cross is called the **origin**. The origin is always labeled 0 on each axis.

Any point on a grid can be named with a pair of numbers called an **ordered pair**. For example, the ordered pair for the origin is (0, 0). When naming a point, always name its position along the *x*-axis first. This number of an ordered pair is the ***x*-coordinate**. The second number of an ordered pair is the ***y*-coordinate**. It names the position of a point compared to the *y*-axis.

For example, look at the upper left corner of the square graphed below. Its position is 3 units to the right of the origin, along the *x*-axis, so its *x*-coordinate is 3. It is 7 units above the origin along the *y*-axis, so its *y*-coordinate is 7. The ordered pair for this point is (3, 7).

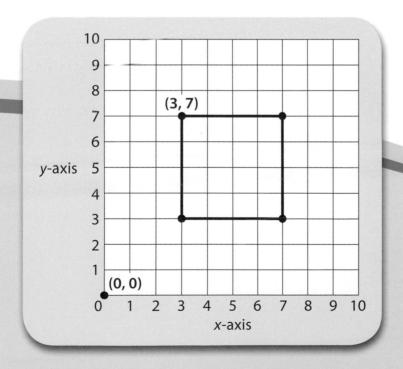

What are the ordered pairs for the other three points on the graph?

Plotting Points: When we graph math data or create a map, we plot points on a grid. That means we place a dot or symbol on the grid. That dot or symbol is placed at the point in which the ordered pair is located.

We frequently plot data in a data table before we make graphs. The table helps us identify relationships between values. Some relationships follow rules. Let's look at these sets of coordinates as an example:

x	1	2	3	4	5
y	1	3	5	7	9

Notice the relationship between the values in each set of coordinates. Each x coordinate is one greater than the coordinate that comes before. So, the rule is +1. Each y coordinate is two greater than the coordinate that comes before. So, the rule is +2. These rules tell us which coordinates come next in the data.

If we plot these numbers on a grid, the graph looks like this:

What would the next coordinate pair be if we followed the same rules?

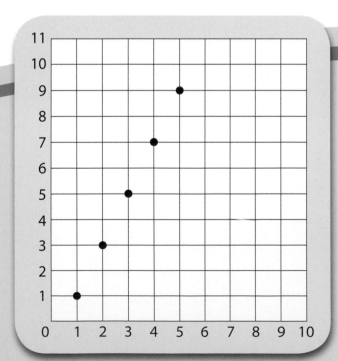

Naming Points: Sometimes, we see objects or symbols on a grid and must use coordinates to locate the object. For example, we find the heart symbol on the following grid and want to know the coordinates at which it is located.

We find the x-coordinate first by following the vertical line down from the heart. We come to the number 1 on the x-axis. Next, we follow the horizontal line left from the heart. We come to the number 1 on the y-axis. This is the y-coordinate. So, the ordered pair for the heart symbol is (1, 1).

 What's the Word?

You may have heard the word *geocaching*. The prefix *geo–* means "earth." The base word *cache* means "a collection of items hidden in a particular place."

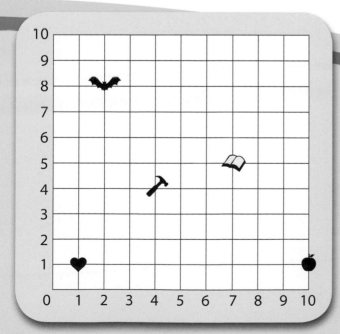

What are the ordered pairs that name the locations of the other symbols on the grid?

9

DISCOVER ACTIVITY

Materials

- measuring tape
- graph paper
- pencil
- masking tape or pieces of string
- math compass

Make a Map Like a Professional

Many people use grid and graph skills in their work. For example, people design gardens for homes, museums, or businesses. Other people design or decorate spaces inside a home or an office.

These professionals usually start with a map or model of the space. They measure the space and may draw where things are, such as bookcases along a wall. Then, they create a grid of where they will put things in the future, such as a desk and chair.

Choose a space inside your home or outdoors. Measure the length and the width of the space. Choose a scale for your drawing. That is, choose the length that one unit on the graph paper will stand for. For example, one square on the graph paper could stand for one square foot in the space you're mapping.

Mark the sides of the space you're mapping. Use tape, pieces of string, or some other material that is easy to remove. These sides in the real space stand for the *x*- and *y*-axes on your map's grid.

Choose an item already in the space to map. It might be a chair in an office or a bush in a garden. Using the pieces of tape or string you laid down, measure the position of the object. Plot the location of the object on your map's grid.

Now, plot the locations of other objects in the space you're mapping. Or, add new objects to the space. Identify their locations from the *x*- and *y*-axes.

Share your grid with a friend or adult. Compare your grid to the actual space your grid represents.

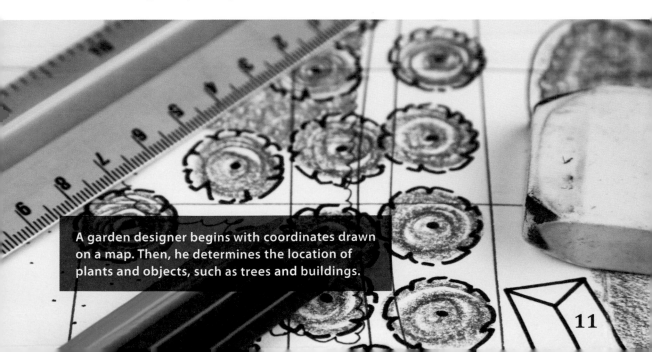

A garden designer begins with coordinates drawn on a map. Then, he determines the location of plants and objects, such as trees and buildings.

Gita's Game

Gita made up the first treasure hunt. She made up clues and puzzles, and she planned where to hide them with each cache. She drew a map of her neighborhood with a coordinate grid marked on it. Then, she borrowed her sister's GPS device. She used buttons on the device to put in the coordinates for each cache.

On treasure hunt day, the team met at Gita's house. She had told her friends to ride their bikes. She handed her friends the map and gave them the GPS coordinates for the first cache. "I'll be waiting at the last cache," she told them. They put the coordinates into the GPS unit, put on their bike helmets, and off they rode!

The coordinates took them to a huge oak tree in a large park at the center of town. Tom spotted the cache in the crook of two branches. Inside the cache were directions and a colorful map. The directions read:

Hang on to this map. You're going to use it again. But for now, find the point on the map marked by the ordered pair (4, 3). Look between the point and the clump of trees on the left. Tell me what animal you see.

What animal is just to the left of (4, 3) on Gita's map?

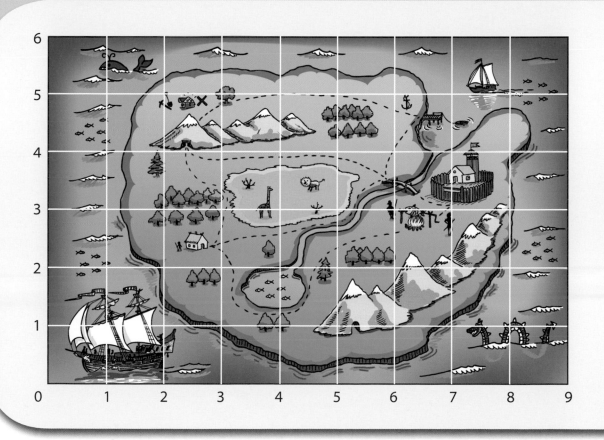

The cache from the oak tree also contained coordinates for Gita's second cache. The friends put these into the GPS device. Then, they pedaled off on their bikes.

Their directions took them to the other end of the same park. When they stopped, they were near a tree and a bench. There was no cache in sight.

Eventually, they found the cache taped to the bottom of the bench. When they opened the cache, they found another set of GPS coordinates and a math puzzle:

Find the rules. Fill in the missing pair.
Then, name the item the numbers declare.

"Okay," said Tom. "Let's figure out what the rules are!" They looked at the data table:

x	7	6	5	4	3	2	—
y	19	16	13	10	7	4	—

Hayden explained, "The *x* rule is simple. Each number is one less than the number before it. So, the rule is 'Subtract 1.'"

"Yes! And I see the *y* rule, too," said Cara.

"I do, too!" said Tom and Marcus at the same time. Tom continued, "Each *y* number is three less than the number before."

The friends found the missing ordered pair quickly, and now they could move on. What was the missing ordered pair?

Look back at Gita's map on page 13. What is located at the point that this ordered pair named?

The friends put the new coordinates into the GPS device and got on their bikes again. This time the GPS guided them out of the park. They rode along a bike path that led back into their neighborhood.

The coordinates brought them to a pole stuck in a rock. The cache was sitting in the grass right next to it. They opened the container and found two more notes. The note marked #1 read, "Where is the sea monster?"

They found the sea monster on Gita's map. They read the *x*-coordinate and *y*-coordinate for the point at the middle of the monster. They wrote down the ordered pair.

What ordered pair names the point at the middle of the sea monster?

Next, the friends opened the note marked #2. They read the following clue:

> Look at the three points you've named on the map.
> What watery space lies in the middle of that?
> Think of a similar place belonging to one of you.
> There, you'll find my last cache and a treat waiting, too.

The friends looked at the map coordinates (4, 2). They decided they were looking for fish in water. Hayden said, "I know! We have a fishpond in my backyard. Let's check there." So, they rode off one more time. A few minutes later they found Gita and Hayden's mom sitting in Hayden's yard. The two waited until the group found the cache floating in the pond. The note inside said, "Chocolate cookies are waiting for you!"

"Hey, everyone!" called Gita. "We made you some cookies!"

"That's great!" said Hayden. "We're hungry after 'fishing' for that last cache. Thank you!"

Marcus' Mystery

The friends chatted while they ate their cookies. Marcus volunteered to organize the next hunt. So, a couple of weeks later, the friends rode their bikes to the town library, where Marcus was waiting.

Marcus handed them only a folded slip of paper. Cara opened the paper and read a pair of GPS coordinates aloud. While Gita put the coordinates into the GPS device, Cara read the rest of the note. It said *Choose yellow*.

"'Choose yellow?" asked Hayden in a puzzled voice.

"That's right. Have fun! See you guys at the end of the hunt," said Marcus.

When Cara, Hayden, Tom, and Gita reached the point marked by their GPS coordinates, they found a cluster of mailboxes.

"Hey," said Tom. "Marcus lives on this road. One of these mailboxes is his."

"Ha," said Gita. "Remember! He said to 'Choose yellow.'" She pointed to the yellow mailbox in the middle. They looked inside and pulled out a plastic bag with two pieces of paper inside.

On one paper, there was a data table with the following instructions.

Find the missing number pair. Be sure to hold onto this paper.

x	0	2	—	6	8	10	12
y	3	5	—	9	11	13	15

The friends quickly figured out the rule. It was the same for both x and y. What is it?

Once they found the rule, the friends filled in chart. What was the missing ordered pair?

The second piece of paper in Marcus' cache had new GPS coordinates. The friends rode on, following the GPS directions. They ended up not far from the mailboxes.

They found a small pile of rocks under some bushes. "Those rocks look out of place," said Hayden. They moved the rocks and quickly found another plastic bag. A paper was inside. The paper turned out to be Marcus' map.

Marcus wrote, "Mark the map with the ordered pair that you found on the data table. Then, find the clump of palm trees on the map. Mark the grid point that touches the tree tops."

What ordered pair names the point touching the top of the palm trees?

It was time to follow the GPS again. The friends put the coordinates they found written on the back of the map into the GPS. Soon after, they stood in front of Tom's house. They stopped near the stairs that led up to the front porch.

After some searching, the friends found a cache under the porch. Inside the little plastic box, they found another note from Marcus. They also found a picture of a lock.

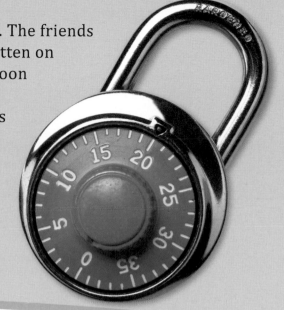

First, look at the map in your possession. Find the point at the top left corner of the treasure chest.

Now you have three coordinates. They make a triangle. What sits in the middle with the body of a lion? Use this clue to find the last cache.

You also need the three coordinates you have found on the hunt so far. Add the digits in each pair of numbers. The three numbers you get will open a combination lock.

Look at Marcus' map again on page 20. What ordered pair names the point to the upper left of the treasure chest on the map?

Next, they looked at each of the ordered pairs. They added the digits in each pair. What three numbers were the results?

Then the friends looked at the three marked points on the map. They thought about the words *body of a lion* for a moment, and quickly realized this must mean the sphinx on the map. They immediately remembered that there was a statue of a sphinx at the town library.

What's the Word?

A *sphinx* (SFINKS) is a mythical creature. It has the body of a lion and the head of a human. There is more than one sphinx in ancient myths. A sphinx in ancient Greece was usually a female who asked riddles. She ate the adventurers who couldn't answer her puzzles. In ancient Egypt, a sphinx was usually a male creature who guarded entrances.

"That takes us back to where we started the day," said Hayden.

Marcus was waiting for them there. A box sat next to the sphinx statue. It had a lock on it.

Hayden, Gita, Tom, and Cara used the three numbers they had and opened the lock. Inside Marcus' last geocache box were five small glass prisms. They were shaped like pyramids.

"One for each of us!" said Marcus. "I saw them in the science toy store in the mall. Aren't they great?"

Everyone agreed. Then, they started planning their next geocache adventure.

MATH AT WORK

There are many large data companies around the world. They collect and sell geographic data. Other companies, such as car and GPS makers, get their data from these companies.

Data companies must keep their data up to date. They hire people to check the facts in person.

The process of comparing GPS maps to places and objects in the real world is called ground-truthing. Data companies have hundreds of employees in many countries around the world. These employees drive all around to check the accuracy of their map data. They check street names, freeway exits, and the locations of streetlights and signs.

To do ground-truthing, employees must have excellent map-reading skills. In other words, they have to be able to read map coordinates and relate them to the real world. They also need to recognize when new places or objects require changes to existing maps.

Maps may have different grids. But that doesn't matter to ground-truthing employees. Their ability to read coordinate grids applies to any map.

Cara's Quest

One afternoon, everyone met to start Cara's geocache hunt. She gave them a map of Africa on a coordinate grid. "This may come in handy," she said, after giving her friends their first set of geocache coordinates. Cara waved as her friends pedaled away.

This is a coordinate map of Africa.

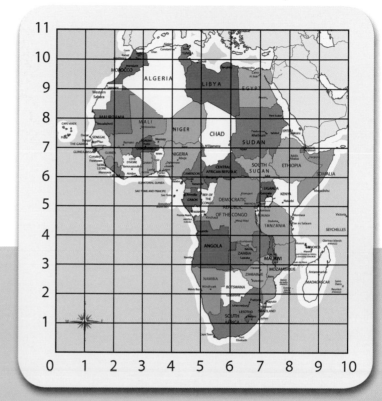

The friends found the first cache behind a bush in front of their school. The message had a question and a clue.

In what country do lemurs live in the wild? The missing coordinates in the data table will help you.

What are the missing coordinates?

x	3	6	—	12	15	18
y	1	2	—	4	5	6

"Madagascar!" Gita shouted.

Ring-tailed lemur and baby

Marcus said, "That's one down!" They took the next set of GPS coordinates from the other side of the paper. Soon, they were on to the next geocache.

A few minutes later, the friends were at home plate on the school's baseball field. Gita remembered that third base came loose. They wiggled it and found the cache underneath.

> Zambia is named for the Zambezi River. This river flows over Mosi-oa-Tunya, one of the largest waterfalls in the world. What waterfall is this? The missing coordinates in the data table will help you.

What are the missing coordinates?

x	3	—	11	15	19
y	2	—	4	5	6

Marcus, Tom, Hayden, and Gita checked the map. Suddenly, Tom said, "Victoria Falls!"

They put the new coordinates into their GPS device and moved on.

Mosi-oa-Tunya is also known as Victoria Falls. It is between the countries of Zambia and Zimbabwe.

Mt. Kilimanjaro is the tallest mountain in Africa. Climbers to the tallest part of the mountain take time to write about their experience in a book. The book is stored in a wooden box stored at the top of the mountain.

The friends soon found themselves at a square in the middle of town. They found Cara's cache tucked in a corner behind a recycling bin. They read the message inside the cache.

This country is famous for photo safaris, acacia trees, and Mount Kilimanjaro. Now, find the missing coordinates.

What are the missing coordinates?

x	1	—	13	19	25
y	0	—	10	15	20

"These coordinates," Gita said, "put us close to a big lake on the map."

"That's Lake Victoria," said Tom. "That's one of the largest lakes in the world, and Mount Kilimanjaro is in Tanzania. So, that's our answer!"

The next GPS coordinates led the friends back around toward the park. They found a different oak tree than on their first treasure hunt. A cache was hidden beneath the leaves of a branch that reached the ground.

The friends read the last clue.

You'll need four sets of coordinates to answer the last question. Here are three of the sets: (7, 3), (7, 4), and (8, 4). Use the data table to find the fourth set. The coordinates form a square around the country you're looking for. Calendar Lake is in this country. The lake, by the way, is 365 miles long and 52 miles wide.

What are the missing coordinates?

x	0	—	16	24	32
y	0	—	6	9	12

"Malawi!" said Hayden, looking at the map.

The friends followed the last GPS coordinates back to the library steps, where they found the last cache. Cara met them at the steps.

Inside the cache were small wall calendars for the next year.

"I get it," said Tom. "Calendar Lake is 365 miles long and 52 miles wide. And there are 365 days and 52 weeks in a year. Cool!"

"Speaking of cool, let's go cool off!" added Tom. They went to a smoothie shop to celebrate finishing another treasure hunt.

Calendar Lake is the nickname for Lake Malawi, seen at sunset in this photograph.

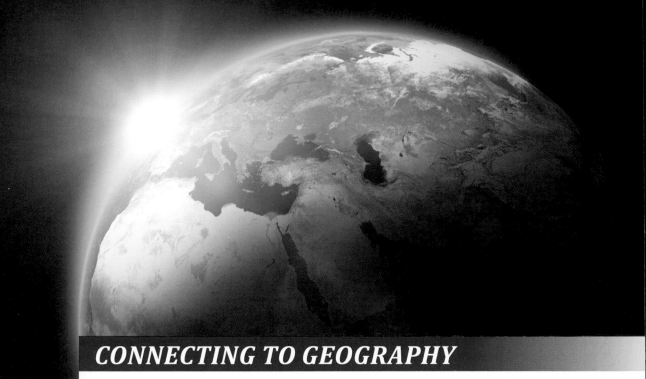

CONNECTING TO GEOGRAPHY

When we look at the world from an airplane or from space, we see no map grid lines or borders between countries. There is only the surface of the planet. The grids we see on maps are entirely imaginary. Humans invented them to plot the locations of land and ocean features.

Planet Earth is a **sphere**, or round shape. People developed a special grid system to map the round object. This grid system uses lines of latitude and longitude.

The equator is an imaginary line that runs around the middle of Earth, along its surface. This imaginary line divides Earth into a Northern and a Southern Hemisphere, or "half-sphere." The surface of a sphere is measured in degrees. The line of latitude we call the equator measures 0°.

Other lines of latitude also run around Earth. Each of these lines runs east and west, **parallel** to the equator. Parallel lines always remain the same distance apart.

This is a map of the South Pole drawn in the 1920s. The South Pole is plotted as a star. Lines of longitude extend like spokes from the star. Lines of latitude make circles around the star.

As Earth rotates, it turns on another imaginary line. We call this line an axis. This axis runs through the center of the planet. The North Pole is located at the north end of this axis. The South Pole is located at the south end.

A straight line is drawn from pole to pole, *over* Earth's surface. This line of longitude is called the prime meridian. It measures 0° and divides Earth into Eastern and Western hemispheres.

Using coordinates of degrees latitude and degrees longitude, we can name any point on Earth's surface. Geographers and mapmakers use these coordinates to create or read maps. Governments use them to define the borders of their countries. And the global positioning system (GPS) uses them to identify locations around the globe.

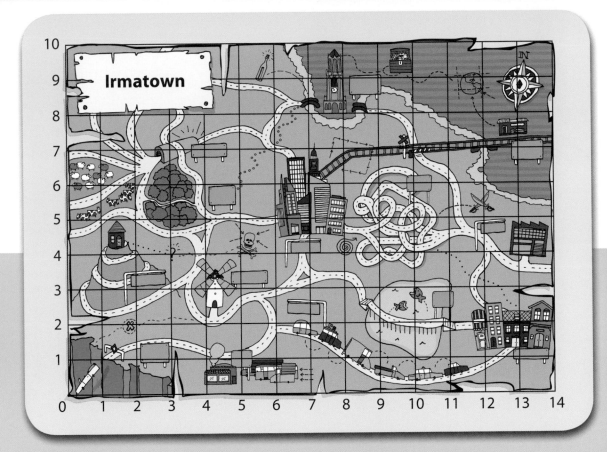

Irmatown

It was Hayden's turn to plan a geocaching tour. She called everyone ahead of time. She wanted to set up a series of geocaches along a hiking trail that she and her family often hiked. It was near town, so they could ride their bikes to the **trailhead**. She and her parents would come along, too.

One morning Cara, Tom, Marcus, and Gita rode their bikes over to Hayden's. They met Hayden and her parents at their apartment. Then, they headed out for the forest trail.

At the trailhead, there were places to lock their bikes. Hayden handed her friends a make-believe map with a grid and a set of GPS coordinates. She also handed out official trail maps for the area, to help them find their way around.

The first set of coordinates took them about a mile down the main trail. Then, they followed a side trail for a short distance. They found the first cache after a few minutes of searching. The following note was inside a small plastic box.

> Look at the map I made. Mark the following coordinates: (1, 4), (1, 5), (2, 4), (2, 5). They form the corners of a square. What do you see inside the square?

What is inside the square marked by the coordinate pairs?

Marcus, Gita, Cara, and Tom answered the question and put new coordinates into their GPS device. Then, they set off again with Hayden and her parents.

Everyone hiked back to the main trail. They followed it until they reached a fork. The GPS coordinates guided them to the left. About one-half hour later, they stopped and began to look for the geocache. They found a small surprise. It was an official geocache! Official geocaches contain a logbook. Players who find a cache can write their names in the logbook and record the time and date they discovered the treasure!

"I went online and found out that there is an official geocache here!" began Hayden. "I got my parents to come out here and find it with me."

Everyone was excited to find the geocache. They opened it, and everyone signed the little logbook inside. Then, Hayden told them they had to find her "unofficial" cache nearby. It contained another clue.

> Look at my map again. Plot the points (6, 5), (6, 7), (8, 5), and (8, 7). What do you see inside the square?

What do you see in the square marked by the coordinate pairs?

The whole group was still chatting about the "official geocache" as they followed the GPS to another cache. They all thought it would be fun to start looking for more official geocaches. Meanwhile, they continued the search for another clue in Hayden's geocache hunt.

Hi, friends! This is the last cache for my hunt. Look at my map again. Plot these points on the map: (4, 2), (4, 4), (5, 2), (5, 4). What you see inside the square is a clue to the last stop for today!

What do you see inside the square marked by the coordinate pairs?

More than 5 million people around the world participate in geocaching. They go online to an official geocaching site to find locations near them or in places they want to go.

Everyone talked for a bit about the image that was meant to be the final clue. They couldn't think of anything like it around town. They were sure they wouldn't find it while hiking in the woods. Suddenly, Gita realized she knew the answer.

"Hayden," Gita asked, "are we . . ."

She didn't need to finish. Hayden was smiling and almost laughing. She simply nodded at Gita, who told everyone she knew where to go. "Back to the bikes," said Gita, and they all hiked back to the trailhead.

They rode to . . . Gita's house! Her family had a miniature windmill in their front yard. It was a garden decoration. But today there were several colorful pinwheels staked into the ground around it. Hayden told everyone to pick a pinwheel and take it home.

Tom's Test

Tom organized the last geocache hunt. They all agreed to meet at the library one more time, since it was central to all their homes. There, Tom gave his friends the first set of GPS coordinates. Then, he waved cheerily as Cara, Gita, Hayden, and Marcus rode away.

The GPS guided them to the side of a soccer field at the edge of the park they had visited already. Once again, bushes were their friend! They found Tom's first cache. Inside it was his map. It was another treasure island, with a coordinate grid drawn on it.

Tom's first cache also held their first math puzzle and another set of GPS coordinates.

Whales are my favorite animals. There are many tales of sea monsters. I think some of those stories must have been whale sightings! Anyway, here's your first clue. Plot the grid point near the middle of the whale on my map!

What ordered pair names the point on Tom's grid in the middle of the whale?

The friends marked the point on the map. Then, they looked at the next coordinates. Cara put them into the GPS device. Off they went!

We call lava that erupts from a volcano magma. In time, magma cools and becomes solid, turning to rock.

Next the group came to a spot across the road from Marcus' mailbox. There was a low stone wall with many dark black rocks in it. They found the cache in a small hole on the back of the wall, where a stone had fallen out.

> Hey, guys! Look at the black rocks in this wall. They originally came from volcanoes, so they were once liquid rock.
>
> ☺ So, your next point to plot is the one nearest the top of the smoking volcano on my map.

Cara was excited about the topic of volcanoes. She turned to look at the volcanic rocks in the wall, while the others discussed what point to mark on the grid. When they had it, they had their next set of GPS coordinates.

What ordered pair on Tom's grid names a point nearest the top of the volcano on the map?

This oasis is in the Sahara Desert in Libya.

About fifteen minutes later, the friends were at a bridge that crossed a small lake in the park. The next cache was tucked under the bridge, only feet away from where they stopped. Inside was another note from Tom.

Okay, last one! Find the missing numbers in the data table. Use them to plot a point on my map. The points make a triangle. What's in the middle of the triangle? Hint: Think of the **mural**, or painting, in town that looks like this part of the picture.

They looked at the data table Tom had made.

x	12	9	—	3	0
y	8	6	—	2	0

What are the missing numbers?

Everyone solved the puzzle at about the same time. They knew their next stop. It wasn't a lake. It was their favorite place to go when they were thirsty. It was a smoothie shop. There is an oasis painted on the side of the shop. An **oasis** is where travelers find water in a desert.

There was a bench outside the smoothie shop. The mural filled the wall behind it.

The friends found the cache hidden beneath the bench. They found a note inside. It read, "Come to my house!"

When they arrived at Tom's, the friends found that all of their families had planned a cookout. The friends and their parents ate and talked about their treasure hunts. They knew this experience was really the beginning. They were all hooked on geocaching!

The group of friends decided to share their geocache adventures with their parents. They all wanted to explain how they used coordinate grids to find treasures. Sometimes they plotted ordered pairs and other times they had to name the points on the grids.

Plotting Points. Tom drew an example of a coordinate grid like the one below. He named the parts of the grid, Parts A–C. Then, he explained how to name the ordered pair marked D.

"A," Tom explained, "is the *x*-axis, B is the *y*-axis, and C is the origin. The ordered pair (0, 0) always marks the origin."

"Now," Hayden jumped in. "Do you see the point marked D? For this point, the *x*-coordinate is 5, and the *y*-coordinate is 9." Hayden traced the lines with her finger. "So, the point at D is the ordered pair (5, 9)."

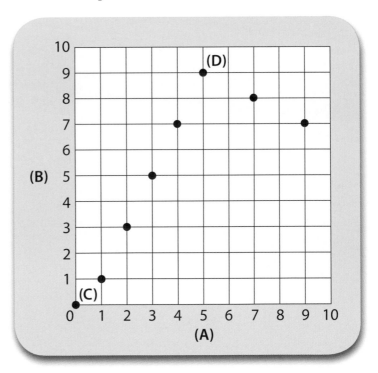

What are the ordered pairs for the other points plotted on the grid?

Naming Points. The friends also wanted to show how they used a coordinate grid to name points.

Gita made the map to the right and explained how to use it. The coordinate grid laid over the map shows locations in their neighborhood.

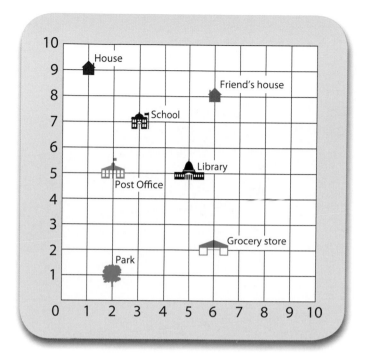

Imagine receiving a clue to find a place on the map. Complete the data table below to find the clue. Then, use the missing numbers as coordinates to locate a place on the map.

x	0	3	—	9	12	15
y	0	4	—	12	16	20

To find the missing numbers in the data table, find the rule for each row. In this case, each number given in a row is greater than the number to the left of it. Find the difference between a number and the number to its left. For the *x* row, the difference between any two consecutive numbers is 3. So, the rule for *x* is "Add 3." The missing *x* value is $3 + 3 = 6$.

For *y*, the difference between any two consecutive numbers is 4. So, the rule for *y* is "Add 4." The missing *y* value is $4 + 4 = 8$.

Use that information to find the missing ordered pair. What is it? What object on the map is plotted at that point?

Consider the coordinate grid to the right. Three figures are plotted on it. Give the ordered pairs for the quadrilateral. The quadrilateral is the four-sided figure.

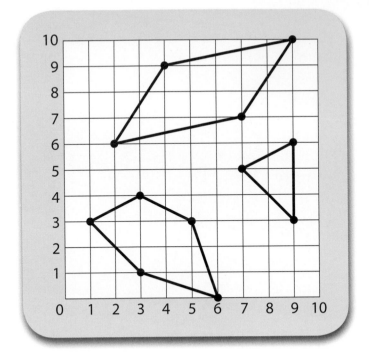

Start by identifying the four ordered pairs for the four corners of the quadrilateral. Begin with any point. Follow a line that passes through the point directly to the x-axis. Find the x-coordinate for that point. Then, look directly left. Follow the line that passes through the point to the y-axis. Find the y-coordinate. Do this for each point.

The four ordered pairs for the quadrilateral are (2, 6), (4, 9), (7,7), and (9, 10).

Now, find the ordered pairs that identify the triangle, or figure with three sides. Then, use what you know to find the ordered pairs that identify the pentagon, or figure with five sides.

There are millions of geocachers around the globe. Gita, Marcus, Cara, Hayden, and Tom have become masters at this game! With your skill at using coordinates to locate places and objects on a map, you can easily become a geocacher just like them. Are you ready for a high-tech adventure of your own?

WHAT COMES NEXT?

Invite an adult to learn more about geocaching with you. Go online to www.geocaching.com to learn about the rules, to find others in your community who participate, and to find the locations of geocaches near you.

Plan a geocaching adventure for your family. Begin by mapping your neighborhood. Find places where you might hide your geocaches. If you need to, check with neighbors to get permission to hide objects in their yards.

Decide what you want to hide in your geocaches. Be sure to include a logbook in each geocache so that your family members can sign the book when they find the treasures you have hidden.

A smartphone works as well as a GPS device. Or your family may have a GPS device already.

Enjoy the adventure with your family. Then, write about your experience. Invite your family members to describe their experiences, too. Have fun sharing your experiences and planning your next adventure!

GLOSSARY

caches: hidden, small waterproof containers that hold treasures.

coordinate grid(s): a 2-dimensional system based on perpendicular number lines.

geocaching: a high-tech, outdoor treasure hunt where players use GPS devices to find caches.

global positioning system (GPS): (1) a satellite-based system used to identify locations on Earth's surface. (2) a device that accesses the global positioning system via satellite.

mural: a painting or other work of art made directly on a wall.

oasis: a green place in a desert, where travelers find water and shade.

ordered pair: a pair of numbers that name a point on a coordinate grid.

origin: the point where the two number lines of a coordinate grid intersect (cross). The origin is always labeled (0, 0).

parallel: a word that describes two lines that never intersect, or cross.

perpendicular: forming a right (90°, or "square") angle.

sphere: a round three-dimensional figure.

trailhead: the beginning of a hiking trail.

***x*-axis:** the horizontal number line on a coordinate grid.

***x*-coordinate:** the first number in a coordinate pair, telling the position of a point relative to the *x*-axis on a grid.

***y*-axis:** the vertical number line on a coordinate grid.

***y*-coordinate:** the second number in a coordinate pair, telling the position of a point relative to the *y*-axis on a grid.

FURTHER READING

FICTION

Geocache Surprise, by Jake Maddox, Stone Arch Books, 2011

Hide and Seek, by Katy Grant, Peachtree Publishers, 2010

Treasure Island, by Robert Louis Stevenson, Penguin Classics, 1999

NONFICTION

Geocaching for Schools and Communities, by J. Kevin Taylor et al., Human Kinetics, 2010

GPS: Global Positioning System, by Jeanne Stunrm, Rourke Publishing, 2009

ADDITIONAL NOTES

The page references below provide answers to questions asked throughout the book. Questions whose answers will vary are not addressed.

Page 7: (3, 3), (7, 3), and (7, 7)

Page 8: (6, 11)

Page 9: bat (2, 8); hammer (4, 4); book (7, 5); apple (10, 1)

Page 13: a giraffe

Page 15: (1, 1). A ship is at point (1, 1).

Page 16: (8, 1)

Page 19: The x-coordinate rule is "Add 2." The y-coordinate rule is "Add 2." (4, 7)

Page 20: (1, 4)

Page 21: (1, 9)

Page 22: 11, 5, and 10 (4 + 7, 1 + 4, and 1 + 9)

Page 25: (9, 3). The x-coordinate rule is "Add 3." The y-coordinate rule is "Add 1."

Page 26: (7, 3). The x-coordinate rule is "Add 4." The y-coordinate rule is "Add 1."

Page 27: (7, 5). The x-coordinate rule is "Add 6. The y-coordinate rule is "Add 5."

Page 28: (8, 3). The x-coordinate rule is "Add 8." The y-coordinate rule is "Add 3."

Page 33: There is a little red house on top of a hill inside the square.

Page 34: There is a group of city buildings inside the square.

Page 35: There is a windmill inside the square.

Page 38: (1, 4)

Page 39: (4, 7)

Page 40: (6, 4). The x-coordinate rule is "Subtract 3." The y-coordinate rule is "Subtract 2."

Page 42: (1, 1), (2, 3), (3, 5), (4, 7), (7, 8), and (9, 7)

Page 43: (6, 8). A friend's house is at point (6, 8).

Page 44: Triangle: (9, 3), (7, 5), (9, 6); Pentagon: (6, 0), (5, 3), (3, 4), (1, 3), (3, 1)

INDEX

CONTENT CONSULTANT

David T. Hughes

David is an experienced mathematics teacher, writer, presenter, and adviser. He serves as a consultant for the Partnership for Assessment of Readiness for College and Careers. David has also worked as the Senior Program Coordinator for the Charles A. Dana Center at The University of Texas at Austin and was an editor and contributor for the *Mathematics Standards in the Classroom* series.